JOURNEY THROUGH

SINGAPORE
a pictorial guide to the lion city

TIMES EDITIONS

Author: Nicolette Yeo
Editor: Nafisah Ismail
Designer: Ang Lee Ming
Picture Researchers: Susan Jane Manuel, Thomas Khoo
Production Co-ordinator: Nor Sidah Haron

© 2003 Times Media Private Limited

Published by Times Editions
An imprint of Times Media Private Limited
A member of the Times International Publishing Group

Times Centre, 1 New Industrial Road, Singapore 536196
Tel: (65) 6213 9288   Fax: (65) 6285 4871
E-mail: te@tpl.com.sg
Online Book Store: http://www.timesone.com.sg/te

Times Subang, Lot 46 Subang Hi-Tech Industrial Park
Batu Tiga, 40000 Shah Alam, Selangor Darul Ehsan, Malaysia
Tel & Fax: (603) 5636 3517   E-mail: cchong@tpg.com.my

National Library Board (Singapore) Cataloguing in Publication Data

Yeo, Nicolette, 1976–
Journey through Singapore / [text, Nicolette Yeo]. – Singapore : Times Editions, c2003.
p. cm. – (Journey through)
ISBN : 981-232-578-6

1. Singapore – Social life and customs. 2. Singapore – Economic conditions.
3. Singapore – History. 4. Singapore – Guidebooks I. Title. II. Series: Journey through

DS609
959.57 – dc21   SLS2003018319

Printed in Singapore by Utopia Press

contents

OVERVIEW

Introduction

Sir Thomas Stamford Raffles founded modern Singapore in January 1819. He deemed the island suitable as a British base and set up a trading post here. Soon after, there was a great influx of immigrants from all over the region in search of work, trade or to escape from war and poverty. Since then, Singapore grew from a small fishing village to a thriving British colony.

Between 1942 and 1945, the British lost Singapore to the Japanese during World War II, but regained it when the Japanese Occupation ended.

ABOVE
Buildings in the central business district (CBD) form an impressive skyline.

RIGHT
A white marble statue of Sir Stamford Raffles stands at the bank of Singapore River to mark his landing site.

TOP
People's Action Party leaders celebrated Singapore's self-government in 1959.

BOTTOM LEFT
Crowds gathered outside City Hall in 1957 for the inauguration of Ong Eng Guan, Singapore's first and only mayor.

BOTTOM RIGHT
Singaporeans protested against a multitude of issues, one of which was the Suitability Certificate, introduced in 1964 to control admission into universities.

The years 1945 to 1959 were crucial ones for Singapore. It was a period of rising nationalism, communism and racial riots. The general instability was aggravated by the ugly threat of Chinese secret societies.

In 1959, the first general election was held in Singapore. It marked the start of self-government under the People's Action Party (PAP), which remains in control until today.

In 1963, Singapore joined Malaya, Sabah and Sarawak to form Malaysia. Singapore, however, had differences with the rest of Malaysia and gained its independence in 1965 with Lee Kuan Yew as prime minister and Yusof Ishak as president. The 1970s and 1980s were periods of great growth and prosperity as Singapore strived to be a successful and prosperous country.

Government and Political Structure

Singapore is a republic and bases its parliamentary system of government on the British Westminster model.

The head of state is an elected president who serves a six-year term. A general election is held every five years to elect parliament members, who are led by the prime minister. President S. R. Nathan won the election in 1999, while Goh Chok Tong has been the prime minister since 1990.

There are a number of registered political parties in Singapore, mainly the People's Action Party (PAP), Workers' Party (WP), Singapore Democratic Alliance (SDA), and the Singapore Democratic Party (SDP). The PAP, however, has dominated the local political scene since the 1960s.

The Supreme Court was opened in 1939 and is located on St. Andrew's Road.

International Image

Singapore is known for having an efficient government and a skilled workforce. The country has been a member of the Association of South East Asian Nations (ASEAN) since 1967 and the United Nations (UN) since 1965.

Singapore has the world's second busiest port and handles more than a million tonnes of cargo every month. Since their early years of operation, the Singapore Changi International Airport (SCIA) and Singapore International Airlines (SIA) have amassed many awards from business and travel magazines worldwide as well as international recognition from foreign travel associations and tourism boards.

Free from corruption, political instability, poverty and natural disasters, Singapore is also known as one of the safest and cleanest countries in the world to live in.

TOP
The CBD during twilight with the Padang in the foreground.

RIGHT
The port of Singapore is located in Tanjong Pagar in the southern part of Singapore.

National Symbols

National Flower

A lovely purple orchid known as the Vanda Miss Joaquim became the national flower in 1981. It was chosen because of its hardy and resilient qualities and ability to bloom throughout the year.

National Flag

The Singapore flag has two equal horizontal sections. The top half of the flag is red while the bottom half is white. Red represents universal brotherhood while white symbolises everlasting purity and virtue. The white crescent moon represents a nascent nation while the five stars feature Singapore's five ideals: democracy, peace, progress, justice and equality.

Pledge

The Pledge was created in 1959. It was originally intended to unify Singaporeans during the troubled times of the 1950s and 1960s, which was a period of political instability and racial disharmony. The Pledge taught people to look beyond race and religion.

National Coat of Arms

The national coat of arms is also known as the state crest. It is a shield that is superimposed by the crescent moon and white stars of the national flag. On the left and right sides of the shield are a lion and a tiger. The lion represents Singapore while the tiger, Malaysia — reminiscent of the fact that Singapore was once part of Malaysia. Below the shield is a banner inscribed with the nation's motto, 'Majulah Singapura', or 'Onward Singapore'.

National Anthem

The national anthem, 'Majulah Singapura', reflects the nation's aspirations for progress and prosperity.

Lion Head Symbol

The lion head has been Singapore's national symbol since 1986. It was introduced as an alternate symbol to the national flag and state crest, which are protected by law against their usage for non-government and commercial purposes. The lion symbolises strength, courage and excellence.

TOP
A cluster of Vanda Miss Joaquim orchids, Singapore's national flower.

ABOVE LEFT
Singapore's national flag was designed in 1959, when the country achieved self-government.

LEFT
Singapore's symbol, the merlion, is a mythical creature that is half mermaid and half lion.

Architectural Icons

Singapore has a number of landmarks that are both of architectural and historical interests.

There are two statues of Sir Stamford Raffles — one in the compound of Empress Place and another at the bank of the Singapore River. The statue at the compound of Empress Place is made of bronze and was inaugurated in 1887 at the Padang. The bronze statue was moved to its present location in 1919. A replica of this statue was made of white marble and placed at the bank of the Singapore River. The marble statue marks the landing site of Raffles when he first set foot on Singapore in January 1819.

The Raffles Hotel was built in the old French Renaissance style but boasts a British colonial ambience — a carryover of its early patrons in the 1900s.

The Istana is Singapore's equivalent of The White House and is where the president resides. The well-proportioned building has Ionic and Doric colonnades, Corinthian pillars, slated roofs and plastered towers.

The Goodwood Park Hotel was formerly known as the Teutonia Club, which served the German expatriate community in Singapore during the colonial years. The South German architecture features ornamental works and a large semi-circular gable end flanking the entrance. The Goodwood Park Hotel is easily recognised by its octagonal tower and pointed tile roof.

TOP RIGHT
A richly-uniformed Raffles Hotel staff stands in front of the old grand dame.

RIGHT
In 1901, the Victoria Memorial Hall was built in memory of Queen Victoria. The bronze original statue of Raffles stands in front of this building.

A recent addition to Singapore's landscape is the Esplanade – Theatres on the Bay, a world-class performing arts centre. It is dubbed the 'durian' because its roof, made of thousands of louvers, bears a startling resemblance to the pungent, thorny fruit of the Southeast Asian region.

TOP LEFT
Chijmes, formerly a Catholic convent, was restored at a cost of S$100 million and is now a popular retail and eatery centre.

LEFT
The Goodwood Park Hotel was built in 1900 and declared a national monument in 1989.

TOP & ABOVE
The Esplanade is located by the Marina Bay waterfront and built at a cost of S$500 million.

The Thian Hock Keng Temple is one of the oldest Chinese temples in Singapore. The building is richly ornamented and has curved roofs and sharp edges decorated with animals of mythical Chinese folklore.

The Sultan Mosque is an arabesque building replete with domes, minarets and balustrades. Designed by a British architect, the mosque's domes have bases that are formed of many glass bottles.

LEFT
The Sultan Mosque was built between 1824–1826 and rebuilt on the same site at North Bridge Road between 1924–1926.

FAR LEFT
Upon safely reaching the shores of Singapore, immgrants from China would immediately show their gratitude at a joss house. The Thian Hock Keng Temple was built on the site of one of the more popular joss houses at Telok Ayer Street.

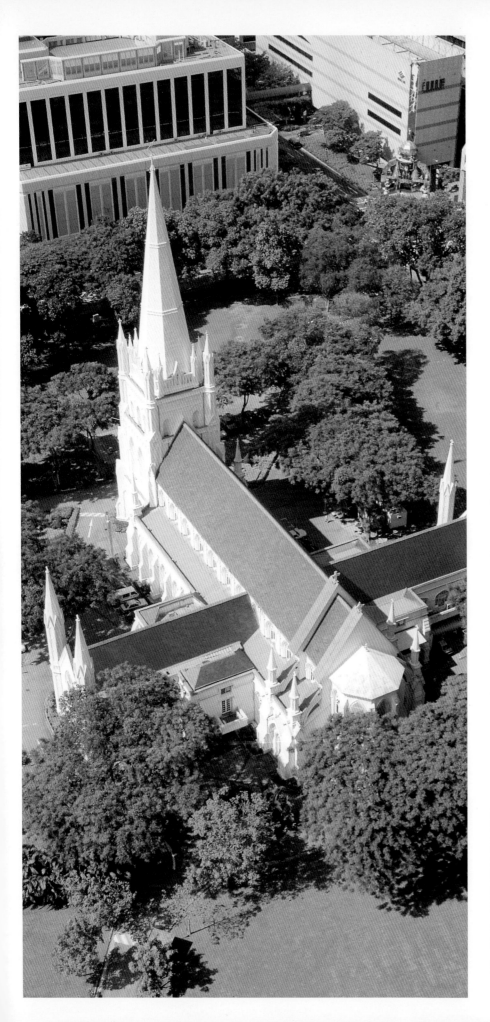

Singapore's oldest Hindu temple, Sri Mariamman Temple, is located at South Bridge Road. The temple has various gods and deities carved on its main structure.

Another religious monument, St. Andrew's Cathedral, has an early English Gothic architecture designed by Colonel Ronald MacPherson of the Madras Army. The cathedral was built in 1856 using Indian convict labour. The outside walls of St. Andrew's Cathedral were plastered with Madras Chunam, which is a mixture of sugar, eggs, lime and coconut husks. This mixture makes the walls glow brightly when polished.

The Victoria Theatre and Victoria Memorial Concert Hall are Singapore's pioneer cultural centres. The latter is built in grand classical British style with graceful pillars and a clock tower.

LEFT
The present-day St. Andrew's Cathedral replaced another church that was built on the same site in 1834.
The original church was struck by lightning twice and finally had to be closed down in 1852.

FAR LEFT
More than just a place of worship, the Sri Mariamman Temple used to provide accommodation to Indian immigrants and served as a Registry for Births and Deaths.

PEOPLE & LIFESTYLE

Population Demographics

Singapore has a population of 4.5 million, with 26.11 migrants for every 1,000 people in the population. The average life expectancy is 80.29 years.

Ethnic Groups

There are four main ethnic groups in the country — Chinese, Malays, Indians and Eurasians. Chinese form the majority at 76.7 percent of the population, while Malays, the second largest ethnic group in Singapore, make up about 14 percent of the population. Indians number 7.9 percent, while Eurasians and other races make up the remainder.

The Chinese

The Chinese in Singapore are made up of many dialect groups, such as Hokkien, Cantonese, Teochew and Hakka. Each has its own dialect. Today, however, most Chinese speak Mandarin as a common platform for conversation among themselves.

The Straits-born Chinese

Peranakan or Straits-born Chinese refers to a group of 'locally born' Chinese, whose forefathers married with local Malay women. As a result, the Peranakans are a separate community of people altogether. They are very different from the other Chinese and

TOP LEFT
Pre-schoolers off to an excursion.

TOP RIGHT
About 75 percent of the population are between 15 and 64 years of age.

have their own language, custom and culture. The Peranakans speak a language known as Baba Malay, which is a mixture of Malay and Hokkien.

The Malays
The Malays are Singapore's original inhabitants. They trace their ancestry to the Bugis from Sulawesi, the Boyanese from Madura in Indonesia, and the Orang Laut, who are descendents of the Sea Gypsies.

The Malays speak Bahasa Melayu, which is the same as Bahasa Malaysia and quite similar to Bahasa Indonesia. Almost all Malays in Singapore profess Islam as their faith.

The Indians
Most of the Indian immigrants were males, causing an imbalance in the Indian population's gender ratio at five males to every one female in Singapore. As a result, many of the single immigrants took Malay women as their wives.

The initial Northern Indian majority was overwhelmed by Southern Indians, who arrived in large numbers and today comprise about 80 percent of the entire Indian population. There are also several smaller groups of Punjabis, Bengalis, Sri Lankan Tamils, Sinhalese, Gujarats and Sindhis.

The Eurasians
A small and often forgotten community, the Eurasians have their roots in the Malay Archipelago when it was under Portuguese and Dutch rule. They are not a single ethnic group but are descendents of a multitude of Asian peoples and Europeans. The term 'Eurasian' is a combination of the words 'Euro' (taken from European) and 'Asian'. The Eurasians' mother tongue is essentially English, although some of the Portuguese Eurasians may still speak a language known as Papia Kristang, which is a mix of Portuguese with Malay grammar.

Religions

The main religions in Singapore are Buddhism, Taoism, Islam, Christianity and Hinduism. The traditional Chinese religions of Buddhism and Taoism account for 51 percent of the population while Islam and Christianity take up 15 percent each. Hindus constitute four percent while the remaining 15 percent is made up of agnostics and atheists.

Buddhism and Taoism

Buddhism revolves around the teachings of the Buddha and Sangha, the monastic order. Most believers follow the Mahayana tradition while others follow the Theravada, Vajrayana and other schools.

Taoism starts with the teachings of Lao Tzu, a sage who believed in 'Tao' or 'The Way'. Its teachings encourage people to live in harmony with nature.

In today's modern society, Singapore Buddhists blend the religion with Taoism and Confucianism, producing a mixture of beliefs, practices and institutions.

Taoists burn joss sticks in temples as they pray. Devotees may also bring food and fruits as offerings.

Islam

The word 'Islam' means 'submission to the will of God', and the believers who so submit are called Muslims. They have the Holy Quran as their guide and are steered by the Five Pillars of the religion. These are to believe that there is no God but Allah and that Muhammad is His Messenger; to pray five times a day; to fast during the month of Ramadhan; to be charitable; and to perform a pilgrimage to Mecca at least once in their lifetime.

ABOVE
Muslims hurry up the stairs to a mosque as the call to prayer is announced.

LEFT
Muslim men congregate for Friday afternoon prayers at a mosque.

An Indian Hindu lady lights lamps for Deepavali, the Festival of Lights.

Christianity

Soon after Sir Thomas Stamford Raffles founded modern Singapore in 1819, Christian missionaries arrived in Singapore to spread the religion. Christianity is based on the idea of Trinity, that God consists of the Father, the Son and the Holy Spirit. There are many subsets under the Christian religion. In Singapore, the Protestant segment is the strongest.

Hinduism

Hinduism advocates that all faiths are different paths to the same God. As the religion teaches of reincarnation, Hindus believe that what people do in the present directly affect what they become in the future.

Other Religions

There are many other religions practiced in Singapore, including Zoroastrianism, Sikhism, Judaism and Jainism.

TOP
Sikh boys in a *gurdwara*, or Sikh place of worship. Here, men and women usually sit at opposite sides of the room.

ABOVE
Being a multireligious society, Singapore holds interreligious prayers or ceremonies during special occasions.

Common Values

Being a multiracial and multireligious society, it is important for all Singaporeans to have common values to bind them together. These values include putting the interests of society ahead of individual interests; giving community support and respect for the individual; treating the family as an important unit; and placing importance in reaching consensus over conflict. Racial and religious harmony are also regarded to be of key importance because they bring about peace and a rich diversity of practices, customs and beliefs to society.

Unique Traits

Singapore has many quirky traits that are worthy of world records.

Kiasuism

Kiasuism is a social religion practiced by the driven in Singapore. In the Hokkien dialect, *'kiasu'* (kiah-SOO) literally means afraid to lose. *Kiasu* Singaporeans desire to be the first or the best in everything they do. Freebies, sales or promotions are typical calls for *kiasu* Singaporeans to manifest themselves. They would even queue overnight or jostle with each other to ensure that they are first in line.

Singlish

Widely used by most Singaporeans, this brand of language is actually English that is liberally peppered with words in Chinese dialects and Malay. This laudable creation has extra exclamatory words such as *'lah'* and *'lor'* at the end of each sentence that has no meaning except to add emphasis.

Chewing Gum Ban

This law became legendary after it was created to stop people with a habit of disposing their chewing gums on lift buttons, public furniture, floors and on the doors of MRT trains, which cause the trains to jam.

Education

Singapore follows the British style of education and requires its students to sit for exams to attain the Ordinary ('O') and Advanced ('A') level certificates.

Compulsory education (CE) was introduced in Singapore in January 2003 when the new school term commenced. The policy makes it compulsory for children who are seven years of age and are Singapore citizens to attend school.

Children begin their educational life in kindergartens at the age of five. Some children begin their education a year earlier at nurseries.

Thereafter, the students study in primary school for six years. They then embark on four or five years of secondary education, at the end of which they take their 'O' level exam.

There are several choices for further education at this point. Students can choose to enter a junior college or an institute and take their 'A' level exam. Otherwise they can opt for diplomas offered by the polytechnics. There are also Institutes of Technical Education, which offer certificates and diplomas geared towards technical fields and information technology.

Finally, there are a variety of degrees, graduate diplomas and certificates offered by local and foreign universities and institutes for students who want to pursue further studies.

TOP LEFT
Kindergarten children put up a performance on stage during their graduation ceremony.

ABOVE LEFT
Students at polytechnics enroll for three-year courses that may range from business to biotechnology, from engineering to nursing, and from banking to shipbuilding.

ABOVE
Every year, students of all ages take part in National Day performances at the Kallang National Stadium.

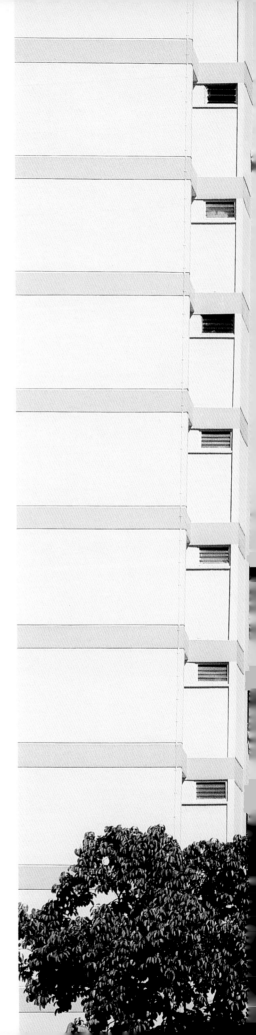

Literacy and Languages

Singapore has four official languages to reflect its diversity – English, Malay, Chinese and Tamil. Malay is the national language and English is the language for business and administration. The literacy rate stands at 93.5 percent, with more literate males than females.

Occupations

Most Singaporeans were employed in the manufacturing sector before the economic downturn. Now about 25 percent of the population is employed in community, social and personal services sector. Other sectors include wholesale and retail, transport and communications, and business and real estate.

National Service

Eighteen-year-old males are required to perform National Service (NS) for a minimum of two years. NS begins with three months of basic military training (BMT). After BMT, the men will be assigned to different units or camps with different vocations. At the end of their training, the men return to civilian life. However, they are required to attend reservist training once a year for the next 13 years of their lives. After that, they will only be recalled in times of need.

TOP & ABOVE
All Singaporean males must serve National Service in the army, navy, air force, police or civil defence.

Residential

The Housing and Development Board (HDB) oversees the purchase, sale, resale and building of public housing known as HDB flats. In Singapore, 86 percent of Singaporeans live in HDB flats. These flats have a price range of S$80,000 to S$500,000, depending on factors such as type, location, size, popularity and floor level.

Only 14 percent of Singaporeans live in private developments, which are mainly apartments and houses. Private developments are very dear, costing from S$600,000 to millions.

LEFT
Clothes hung out to dry on bamboo poles from the back of a HDB block of flats.

ABOVE
The interior of a typical HDB flat.

This shop at Holland Village sells a wide variety of local and international publications that cater to a diverse range of interests.

Transportation

Public transport is the most common form of transportation in Singapore. It is more affordable than private transport and is highly efficient. Public transport include the Mass Rapid Transit (MRT) trains, taxis, bus services, and premier services such as limousines or Bus Plus minibuses. In addition, there are trishaws and rental vehicles.

The cost of private vehicles, particularly cars, are very expensive. A potential vehicle owner has to bid for a certificate of entitlement (COE) before he can purchase a vehicle.

Mass Media

There are two major media players in the country. The Singapore Press Holdings Group and the Media Corporation of Singapore (MediaCorp), own major newspapers, magazines, television channels and radio stations. Singapore's only one pay-TV company, Starhub Cable Vision, offers a choice of over 45 channels.

Until late 2002, the Ministry of Information, Communications and the Arts (MITA) issued licenses for films, publications and television and oversaw media and arts issues. The Media Development Authority, a new statutory board, has taken over these duties.

Celebrities

Despite a very young entertainment industry, Singapore has produced several quality entertainers.

Stefanie Sun

The fresh-faced songbird became an instant hit with her debut Mandarin album *Cloudy Days*. Since then, she has created a storm with chart-topping songs, record breaking sales, numerous music awards and sellout concerts in Taiwan and Singapore.

Zoe Tay

Zoe Tay was first discovered when she won a talent search contest conducted by the Singapore Broadcasting Corporation (now MediaCorp). Her acting skills and elegant bearing landed her leading roles in local productions. She has long been acknowledged as the most popular Chinese actress in Singapore.

Lim Kay Tong

Famed for his stage appearances, Lim Kay Tong has had some success on foreign shores. He has appeared in Hollywood movies such as *Brokedown Palace, Dragon: The Bruce Lee Story* and *It Could Happen To You.*

ECONOMIC
LANDSCAPE

Main Industries

The economy is driven by electronic products and components manufacturing, refined petroleum products and chemicals as well as chemical products. Other significant industries are fabricated metal products manufacturing, machinery and equipment manufacturing, transport equipment manufacturing, petrochemicals and petrochemical products.

Seaport

The port of Singapore is a focal point for some 400 shipping lines with links to more than 700 ports in 130 countries worldwide. The port offers a host of services that include cargo handling, warehousing, distribution, bunkering and ship supplies. In addition, it provides 24-hour security, environmental control and fire fighting. The port has a total of six terminals that can accommodate all types of marine vessels.

LEFT
The port of Singapore is one of the world's busiest, but it is facing competition from new ports in neighbouring countries.

ABOVE
Production workers check microchips through microscopes in an electronics and technology centre.

Financial Business Districts

The CBD is in Shenton Way, where big international names jostle cheek and jowl with local ones.

Shopping Areas

There are several shopping belts spread across the island for different shopping preferences.

Orchard Road is the main shopping strip. It has department stores, shops, designer boutiques, supermarkets, game arcades, cinemas and a wide array of food and beverage outlets. The City Link Mall is a subterranean mall linking Raffles City Shopping Centre with the Marina Centre area, another premier shopping belt.

Slightly off east is Bugis Junction, famed for its Japanese goods as well as its night market. The night market is a bargainer's paradise full of trendy batik wear, compact discs, fruits, shoes, leather products and other knick-knacks.

The Millenia Walk area is where one can find Harvey Norman, a megastore selling everything from furniture to bedding, and from communications to electronics equipment.

Chinatown is a haven for lovers of Oriental things such as Chinese outfits, birds' nests, ginseng, jade and bronze figurines, embroidery, porcelain, wood carvings and cultural artifacts.

From music, movies to fabrics, made-in-India products are receiving international acclaim. Little India has a gamut of quaint shops displaying sarees, Hindi movie posters, flower garlands, exotic herbs and spices and Indian delicacies.

LEFT
The Elgin Bridge spans across the Singapore River. The new Parliament House is the red-roofed building at the extreme left.

BELOW LEFT TO RIGHT
Traditional Chinese medical halls still flourish in Singapore; The underground City Link Mall is a popular place for shopping and hanging out; Stalls are set up outside Ngee Ann City at Orchard Road to catch the weekend crowd; Trees provide shaded relief for pedestrians strolling along Orchard Road.

Geylang Serai is home to the Malay community and boasts hordes of ethnic clothing, fragrant spices, handicrafts and scrumptious Malay food.

Arab Street offers a dazzling visual feast of handmade straw products, silks, garments, trinkets, beads and many other handmade items. Be prepared to bargain, however, for the merchants expect it.

Foreign Talent
Singapore is a country with no natural resource. As such, its only resource is human capital. The employment of foreign manpower enables Singapore to grow beyond its limited resources. As part of a national effort to enhance Singapore's competitiveness, the Ministry of Manpower is constantly attracting foreign talent to fill specific gaps and roles in the economy. In addition, there is a total foreign worker management system to allow foreign workers to maximize their economic contribution to Singapore.

Technology
Technology serves to improve lives by making them more efficient, convenient and varied. About three in five homes in Singapore have at least one computer, with an increasing number of homes having more than one computer. Singapore also has one of the highest Internet usage rates in the world, with nearly half of the population accessing the worldwide web.

Mobile phones used to be a status symbol but today are more of a necessity. About 73 percent of the population are mobile phone users, making Singapore a country with one of the highest mobile phone penetration rates in the world.

LEFT
Cheerful Malay vendors prepare food in the late afternoon to get ready for break fast at sunset. Stalls like these are set up in the Geylang Serai area during Ramadhan, adding to the festive air.

CLOCKWISE FROM TOP LEFT
Baskets and other rattan goods are aplenty at Arab Street; A Caucasian, one of the many foreign workers in Singapore, relaxes over a cup of coffee on a Sunday; A man tries out the wireless Internet service at a cafe. Customers of Singtel, the nation's primary communications provider, can enjoy wireless broadband Internet access at over 100 wireless surf zones; People surfing the Internet at a cybercafe; A Little India stall sells flower garlands, which are used in Hindu worship activities.

ARTS & LEISURE

TOP
Chijmes comes alive with beautiful lighting
and alfresco diners in the evening.

ABOVE
Two joggers at the MacRitchie Reservoir.
Jogging is one of the more popular
fitness activities in Singapore.

Major Hobbies

Eating is a major hobby for Singaporeans. With the multitude of hawker centers, food courts and 24-hour eating establishments, many Singaporeans spend their weekends scouring for the best bites.

Shopping is another national pastime as there is always a sale going on somewhere. Many weekends are spent scouting around for bargains, designer goods and plenty more.

Education and affluence has stressed the importance of taking care of one's body, thereby making sports another popular hobby.

Watching movies is a form of entertainment enjoyed by the young and old alike. The main action is concentrated in city areas, although many suburban malls have cineplexes, which are complexes containing several cinemas.

Local interest in the arts has shown a slow but steady increase. There are a myriad of arts activities that offer something for everyone, from local exhibitions and plays to world-class performances.

Activities and Sports

The most popular sport in Singapore is football. Every year, the Football Association of Singapore (FAS) organizes the S-League, which consists of 12 local teams.

Other popular sports include badminton, table tennis, squash, golf and bowling. Families usually cycle and swim together. Fitness centers and gyms are popular with the health-conscious. The young and more adventurous engage in mountaineering, rock climbing, powerboating, waterskiing and wakeboarding. There are also defence sports such as silat, karate, judo, wushu and taekwondo.

Sports native to the cultural groups in Singapore include *sepak takraw* – a ball game played mainly by the Malays which involves kicking a round ball made out of wooden strips.

The Chinese engage in a sport known as dragon boat racing that involves racing on canoe-like boats with dragon carvings during the Mid-Autumn Festival.

LEFT FROM TOP
Dragon boats may be up to 100 feet long, but they are very narrow and only two people can sit side by side in them; Singapore has windsurfing clubs which hold competitions on a regular basis; The beach is also a favourite place for people to exercise, cycle and jog.

ABOVE
Soccer is a favourite sport and brings people of various races together.

Theatre and Drama

Theatre is the most popular type of performing arts in Singapore, which is presented in the four official languages. The theatre scene has undergone an exciting phase since 1988, with the emergence of new ideas and experimental theatre groups. It is now capable of producing plays of high artistic quality, experiment with modern and traditional forms and infuse the various language streams. It explores both local issues and universal themes, giving them recognition in the region and all over the world.

Music

From traditional Chinese orchestras to jazz, funk or rock bands, symphonic bands to military bands, and classical guitar ensembles to female pipers, Singapore serves a wide range of musical tastes. There are even orchestras featuring native Indonesian instruments called the *angklung* (ANG-klong) and *gamelan* (gah-MAY-lahn), and a Chinese instrument called the *guzheng* (GOO-cheng). In addition, there are music societies, school bands, entertainment bands and professional musicians. Singapore has also produced a number of singers who are known regionally, such as Kit Chan and Hetty Sarlene.

RIGHT
Chinese opera used to be popular. Today, however, it is mainly performed during the Seventh Month festival.

FAR RIGHT FROM TOP
The Singapore Chinese Orchestra has performed in countries such as China and Egypt; Singapore holds local plays and hosts performances by international theater groups regularly.

Popular Hangouts

The republic is an urban jungle alive with swanky eateries, posh clubs and hip cafes. Orchard Road is a perennial favourite with locals and tourists alike. Singapore's largest shopping belt also houses enclaves of bars, pubs, clubs and casual and fine dining establishments. This strip offers quaint bric-a-brac shops alongside designer labels such as Prada and Gucci.

Boat Quay was Singapore's first club strip. Nightspots range from jazz clubs to rock clubs, and chill out bars to karaoke bars. Restaurants along Boat Quay offer an eclectic range of Thai, Chinese, Indonesian, North Indian, Irish and local cuisines.

Clarke Quay, Singapore's only festival village, is home to a bevy of food and beverage outlets. There are pushcart stalls and shops, along with a vanishing trades centre. At the center of Clarke Quay is a gazebo where free performances are staged occasionally.

Mohammed Sultan Road is a strip of watering holes housed in pre-war shophouses. Word has it that many tortured souls still roam their former abodes. However, the only spirits one will see when one gets here are of the human kind, very often lifted by one too many pints of beer.

Club Street is a relatively new kind of entertainment hangout. The street is aptly named considering the upmarket drinking establishments and eateries mushrooming all over the otherwise quiet area.

Formerly the site of a convent school for girls, Chijmes (pronounced Chimes) is now a vibrant, bustling enclave of watering holes, casual and fine dining establishments and a world-famous club – China Jump. Asian food takes a backseat as the cuisine on offer is decidedly Western.

The Esplanade – Theatres on the Bay and the Merlion Park are the newest chill-out areas. Although lavish eateries and watering holes are aplenty in both areas, the real attraction is the impeccable view of the Merlion statue set against a backdrop of huge skyscrapers overlooking a tranquil river.

The beach is a popular location for family picnics, water sports and events. It is a sanctuary for couples seeking privacy, as much as it is an exciting place for groups seeking fun.

ABOVE
A family spends a weekend by having a picnic at the beach.

CLOCKWISE FROM TOP RIGHT
Boat Quay throbs at night; A juggler entertains bystanders during the opening of the Esplanade in October 2002; People unwind at a Raffles City cafe.

Other Places of Interest

Jurong Bird Park
This sprawling, beautifully landscaped park is home to over 8,000 birds. The park also houses the world's tallest man-made waterfall.

Jurong Crocodile and Reptile Paradise
Set in a lush tropical landscape, this park features crocodiles, snakes, iguanas, chameleons and giant tortoises.

Singapore Zoological Gardens
Billed as one of the best zoos in the word, the zoo blends its 2,800 animal residents with various plants and trees. It offers an open zoo concept where animals are free to roam in the safety of their own enclosures that are modeled after those in the wild.

Underwater World
This oceanarium is the largest in Asia. There is also a Dolphin Lagoon on the Central Beach of Sentosa Island, where people can swim alongside Indo-Pacific Humpback Dolphins, also known as Pink Dolphins.

Night Safari
The world's first and only night safari combines a zoo and a national wildlife park quite unlike its African counterpart, as the main activities take place after dark. It is home to more than 1,200 animals of over 110 exotic species.

FAR LEFT
The Singapore Zoological Gardens' famed orang utans in their enclosure, which is modelled to resemble the orang utans' natural habitat.

ABOVE LEFT
A white pelican roams free at the Jurong Bird Park.

LEFT
Visitors to the Night Safari get to view the nocturnal activities of animals such as tigers, jackals and giraffes.

A pair of cable cars ply between the main island and Sentosa at sunset. Apart from cable cars, visitors can get from Singapore to Sentosa and back via bus or private vehicle.

Museums

Singapore's museums showcase the heritage of the region and that of the early Chinese immigrants. It also has on display contemporary art, historical artifacts, documents charting Singapore's history and a unique collection of stamps and first day covers.

Snow City

Made possible by 150 tonnes of manmade snow, the Snow City has attractions that include a snow slope, snow play area, ski lodge cafe and a subzero exhibition. Besides these, the more adventurous can try snowtubbing, skiing and snowboarding.

Singapore Science Centre

The centre is home to Singapore's premier Omni-Theatre, which plays IMAX large format films. The centre is also touted as one of the top science centres in the world. It displays over 650 interactive exhibits in various theme halls to provide high quality education and entertainment.

Singapore Discovery Centre

The centre is a place for visitors to see, hear, touch and discover Singapore's milestones and achievements through interactive and high technology exhibits. The Singapore Discovery Centre has a giant screen for 3D and 2D shows, motion simulator rides, shooting gallery, tunnel of illusions and visual dynamics theatre.

Sentosa Island

Just half an hour away from the main city is Singapore's only island resort. This self-contained island plays host to a musical fountain, hotels, food and beverage establishments, museums, heritage trails, historical monuments and beach bars.

Escape Theme Park

Singapore's answer to Disneyland has roller coasters, go-karts, wet slides and bumper boats. In addition, there are carnival stalls with games, food and lots of action.

Prominent Artists

In the early years, the only form of entertainment enjoyed by the many immigrants was Chinese street opera. Today's artists have come a long way from painted faces and sordid lives and have made sizeable contributions to the arts in Singapore.

Kuo Pao Kun

Widely acknowledged as the father of Singapore theatre, the late Kuo Pau Kun dedicated his life to raising the profile of performing arts. For 20 years he actively wrote and directed plays in Mandarin and English, conducted theatre workshops and introduced local theatre practitioners to China, Taiwan and Hong Kong theatres.

Glen Goei

Having starred in the acclaimed *Madam Butterfly* and acted opposite Anthony Hopkins, Glen Goei has perhaps made the greatest mark for a Singaporean thespian. He currently runs Wild Rice Productions, a theatre company that produces contemporary dramas.

Lee Huei Min

This child prodigy played violin in the Singapore Symphony Orchestra at the tender age of 12. Since then, she has received accolades on the local and international classical music scenes, and has played at numerous concerts and national events. She has recorded her first album with the London Symphony Orchestra.

CLOCKWISE FROM ABOVE LEFT
An exhibit at the Singapore Museum displays a typical living quarter for Chinese immigrants when they first came to Singapore; The Substation was founded by Kuo Pao Kun and is home to the arts in Singapore; A skydiving simulation machine at the Singapore Discovery Centre gives visitors the thrill of the sport without the dangers.

RIGHT
The Mother and Child sculpture by Ng Eng Teng, a respected local sculptor, sits outside Far East Shopping Centre in the Orchard Road belt.

A stall selling Chinese New Year decorations. Red is the favoured colour among the Chinese as it is a symbol of good luck and prosperity and is believed to offer protection against evil.

HOLIDAY
SEASONS

Religious Festivals
Chinese New Year

This event celebrates the new year according to the Chinese calendar. Red pieces of paper bearing wishes in Chinese calligraphy are proudly displayed on doors and walls. A reunion dinner on the eve of the new year brings family members together, while it is customary for the Chinese to visit the houses of relatives and friends on the first and second days. Red money packets are given to the unmarried as a gesture of good fortune.

Qing Ming Festival

This is a Chinese festival that is observed in early April. Qing Ming remembers ancestors and the recently deceased. On this day, families visit graves and clear the site of unwanted plants. They then light candles and joss sticks and give offerings of food and wine.

The Chinese honour the dead on Qing Ming by visiting the tombs and columbariums of their dear departed. Entire families visit to clean the sites and give offerings.

Yu Lan Jie Festival

Commonly called the Festival of the Hungry Ghosts or Seventh Month Festival, this event serves to honour the dead. It is believed that on this day, the gates of hell are open and spirits roam the earth. The Chinese place food and offerings of burnt hell money and paper goods for the dead at roadsides. Chinese opera shows entertain the spirits and the living.

Mid-Autumn Festival

Yet another popular Chinese festival is the Mid-Autumn or Mooncake/Lantern Festival. This is celebrated by eating mooncakes with a variety of sweet and savoury fillings. The mooncakes signify unity and a cycle completed. Children carry colourful plastic or paper lanterns of all shapes and sizes during the night.

ABOVE
Lanterns are set afloat on a pond in the Chinese Garden during the Mid-Autumn Festival.

RIGHT
Chinese offer gigantic candles like these, along with food and paper money, during the Hungry Ghost Festival.

Hari Raya Puasa

This a festival celebrated by Muslims at the end of Ramadhan, the Islamic fasting month. Muslims attend special prayers at mosques in the morning and then have a meal with family members. The event is also celebrated by visits to the homes of relatives and friends. Children receive gifts of money, which are placed in little envelopes.

Hari Raya Haji

Muslims who can afford it make the pilgrimage to Mecca during this period. The event is also marked by the sacrifice of goats or cows, whose meat are distributed to the needy.

ABOVE
On Hari Raya Puasa, Muslims seek each others' forgiveness for the wrongs they did in the past year.

LEFT
Muslims throw their doors wide open to friends of other races and religions, especially during Hari Raya, for feasting and merriment.

Tamil New Year

This event ushers in the new year according to the Tamil calendar. Hindus rise early for a ritual bath and worship ceremony at the family shrine. This is followed by visits to the temple and homes of family and friends. The Hindu almanac, which lays down the positions of the planets and stars, is published at this time.

Thaipusam

Thaipusam is one of the most intriguing Hindu festivals and celerabtes faith and endurance. Devotees travel from one temple to another carrying the *kavadi* in penitence or thanksgiving. The *kavadi* is a special wooden arch with a base. It is decorated with peacock feathers and supports various offerings of fruits, flowers and milk. Some devotees carry the metal *kavadi* that is affixed by sharp skewers driven through their tongues, cheeks and bodies.

Thimithi

The amazing fire-walking ceremony, or Thimithi, has devotees walking on burning coals barefooted. This ceremony honours Draupathi, who had to prove her innocence by walking on burning coals.

Deepavali

Deepavali, or the Festival of Lights, is an occasion of much rejoicing by the Hindus and Sikhs. It symbolises the victory of good over evil, and light over darkness. It is also believed that souls of the departed descend to earth, hence devotees often light lamps to guide these benevolent spirits on their journey back to the next world.

ABOVE
A Deepavali ceremony takes place in a temple. In Hinduism, fire and light are symbols of enlightenment and purity.

LEFT
A young child is dressed up to participate in the Thaipusam processions. The festival celebrates the birthday of Lord Subramaniam, the youngest son of Hindu god Shiva.

FAR LEFT
A *kavadi* is secured to this devotee using skewers.

Vesak Day

Vesak Day denotes perfection and recognises the birth, enlightenment and Nirvana of the Buddha. Buddhists honour the occasion with chants, recitations and offerings at shrines. They also release captive animals, usually birds, on Vesak Day. Temples are colourfully decorated with flags, lights and flowers. There are mass candlelight processions accompanied by chanting. The highlight of the festival is a gathering of devotees at a major public theatre with religious and cultural performances.

Christmas

Christians around the world honour the birth of Jesus Christ during Christmas. Churches hold special mass on the eve and on the day itself. The majority of Singaporeans take this opportunity to admire the lighted decorations at Orchard Road, go out with friends and generally have fun.

Good Friday and Easter

Good Friday is a solemn festival marking the trial and crucifixion of Christ, marked by special church mass. The following Sunday is Easter Sunday which remembers Christ's resurrection.

Non-Religious Festivals

There are many festivals in Singapore that are enjoyed by everyone. These serve to unite Singaporeans as a whole.

National Day

The nation's birthday falls on August 9 and is gazetted as a public holiday. National flags and buntings are proudly displayed on the walls and doors of buildings. The highlight of the day is the National Day Parade, which features a smorgasbord of performances on a grand scale at Kallang National Stadium.

FROM TOP
Buddhists celebrate Vesak Day by congregating in a temple. The lit candles will be carried by devotees in a procession; Orchard Road is set alight with decorations during the Christmas season; A rapt audience listens to music performances by Trilok Gurtu, an Indian musician, at Fort Canning Park during the 2001 WOMAD festival.

Singapore Arts Festival

The Singapore Arts Festival brings together great local and overseas works and artists. The festival begins with performances at the Festival Village, where tribal and folk music and dance from all over the world come together. These acts are accompanied by ethnic crafts and cuisine. Every year, there are about 80 performances by over 30 groups.

Great Singapore Sale

The annual shopping extravaganza is set to woo shoppers locally and regionally. Usually held from May to July, stores all over the island offer up to 70 percent discounts on their goods.

Singapore Food Festival

Every year between March and April, there are mini-food festivals, events and promotions held at various locations to celebrate the nation's favourite pastime.

The Singapore River Buskers' Festival

The banks of the Singapore River come alive with acrobats, musicians, stuntmen, human statues, fire-eaters, magicians and all manner of street performances every November.

WOMAD Singapore

WOMAD is a festival of music, visual arts and dance which bring together international talents. Its aim is to excite and inform, and make more people aware of the worth and potential of a multicultural society.

Singapore International Film Festival

Another festival of artistic value, the Singapore International Film Festival promotes film as an artistic medium in Singapore. The festival was launched in 1987 and screens about 300 award-winning and critically acclaimed films from over 45 countries. In addition, there are workshops, seminars and exhibitions on film-making.

TOP & ABOVE
Chingay processions add excitement to Chinese New Year celebrations. The processions began in 1973 and have been held every year since.

LEFT
Chefs from around the world prepare food for the World Gourmet Summit, which is held in conjunction with the Singapore Food Festival.

Two ladies enjoy the food at a Chinese restaurant with a warm atmosphere.

FOOD

Cuisine

It has been said that in Singapore, one can eat different dishes, three meals a day for 365 days a year and still not have tasted every dish there is.

There is almost every dish under the sun in Singapore, including home-grown favourites such as Indian curries, a wide range of Chinese delicacies, Malay and Indonesian specialties, Singapore's own food innovations and Straits Chinese cuisine, which is a unique mix of Malay and Chinese fare. All of these can be found together with nouvelle cuisine from France, sushi from Japan, tacos from Mexico and pasta from Italy.

Dining Experiences

On a daily basis, Singaporeans converge at hawker centers that are found at every corner of Singaporean streets. These are open-air food centres that offer a variety of local cuisine. Food courts, often found in shopping centres and suburban malls, offer the same fare as the hawker centres but in air-conditioned comfort.

Indoor or alfresco coffee houses and cafes serve anything from local cuisine to sandwiches and steaks. One step up is the casual dining outlet. They are either specifically catered to a particular cuisine or offer Asian, Western and local fare.

Finally, there is the fine dining restaurant which offers specialty cuisines, classy ambience and fine tableware at dearer prices.

TOP
Indian ladies in sarees enjoy lunch at a hawker centre.

LEFT
Food courts are aplenty in Singapore and offer food that may range from Korean to Indian and Western to Middle Eastern.

Uniquely Singaporean Dining Experiences

The Lau Pa Sat Festival Market has a special place in the hearts of Singaporeans. This is where they can feast on local delights alfresco. What is unusual is the fact that pushcart hawkers whip up their wares by the roadside, so patrons can literally dine on the street.

Equinox Complex offers the best view of Singapore's impressive skyline. The restaurant and bar complex is located at levels 68 through 72 of Swissotel the Stamford Hotel in Raffles City, and serves drinks and fine food.

Singaporeans also enjoy Chinese delicacies at Prima Tower, one of the country's few revolving restaurants.

Dining with animals is another unusual experience in Singapore. The Singapore Zoological Gardens allow visitors to have breakfast or tea with one of its orang utan, Ah Meng.

TOP
Lau Pa Sat is famed for its satay, which is grilled outdoors over charcoal fire.

ABOVE
Food signs stating dishes and prices clamour for patrons' attention.

At Bugis Village, enjoy lobster and other seafood dishes in an outdoor setting.

TOP
Food courts provide air-conditioned comfort from the sultry heat.

ABOVE & LEFT
Durians and rambutans are popular tropical fruits. People shake, tap and sniff at the durians to gauge their quality.

National Favourites

Many will consider that Singapore's national dish is the chili crab. Huge Sri Lankan crustaceans are fried to perfection in a thick, spicy, chili gravy. The fresh taste of the crabs is as delightful as mopping up the gravy with French loaves or fried buns.

Chicken rice is easily Singapore's most popular dish. It is a combination of chicken steeped in hot liquid, splashed with a touch of sesame oil and soy sauce, rice cooked in chicken stock and an aromatic chilli-garlic sauce.

Noodle dishes such as wonton noodles, fried flat vermicelli and fishball noodles are also extremely popular. Roti prata is another favourite. It is a flat, round Indian pancake made of dough and fried to a crisp accompanied by delicious curries.

Taboos and Beliefs

There are many accompanying food taboos and beliefs that are practiced by devotees of the different religions.

Muslims do not eat pork. The meat Muslims eat must be *halal,* which means the animals must be slaughtered in a certain manner. Hindus believe that cows are sacred animals, hence they do not eat beef. Many Taoists also do not eat beef. This is according to the teachings of Lao Tzu. Some Buddhists and Taoists practice vegetarianism. Although Buddha never prevented his followers from eating meat, he preached the sins of killing.

Feasts

Although they eat round the clock, Singaporeans generally feast during festive occasions.

The reunion dinner held on the eve of Chinese New Year is an occasion for great feasting. This usually comprises the best Chinese fare. A special dish, called raw fish salad, is believed to bring good luck for the new year as fish symbolises wealth and prosperity. Visits to the homes of friends and relatives during this period is also accompanied by dining on sweetmeats, crisps, biscuits, cakes and sweets.

During the Mid-Autumn festival, the Chinese eat mooncakes, which are round cakes filled with red bean and lotus seed paste with egg yolks.

Hari Raya Puasa is also celebrated by visits to the homes of friends and family. This is accompanied by grand feasting on a variety of Malay dishes, such as ketupat and lontong (compressed rice), meat curries, cakes, cookies, candies and desserts.

Similarly, Hindus and Sikhs celebrate Deepavali by feasting and visiting family and friends. Food includes spicy rice dishes and curries, as well as sweet cakes and candies.

During Vesak Day, vegetarian food is served free at temples as a mark of respect to Buddha's teachings.

FAR LEFT FROM TOP
Hari Raya goodies such as pineapple tarts and chocolate almond cookies are stored in stacks of cookie containers; During Chinese New Year, raw fish salad must be tossed high for more luck.

TOP
Coconut leaves are woven to form packets, which are then filled with rice grains. These are cooked for several hours over a slow fire to form *ketupat*.

LEFT
Mooncakes are eaten during Mid-Autumn festival, which traditionally celebrates the harvest festival.

NATURE

Geographical Landscape
Singapore is located in Southeastern Asia between Malaysia and Indonesia. Singapore has a total land area of 692.7 square km comprising the main island and numerous islets scattered to its northeast and south.

Singapore's terrain is lowland with a gently undulating central plateau containing water catchment areas and nature reserves. Due to its small size and flat terrain, its highest point is a mere 166 m above sea level. About 87 percent of the land is built up for residential and commercial use.

A man admires the sunset at a reservoir. Reservoirs in Singapore are often surrounded by nature reserves.

Weather

Being a tropical island, Singapore is generally very hot and humid and occasionally rainy. Temperatures have an average range of 26°C and 31°C. Thunderstorms occur on 40 percent of all days and annual rainfall stands at 2,345 mm.

The republic also experiences the monsoon season, which produces rainy days, thunderstorms and stormy waters. Higher temperatures and lower rainfall characterise the southeast monsoon occurring from June to September. November to January is when the northeast monsoon takes place. Temperatures are generally cooler with higher rainfall.

Landscaping

Besides its reputation as a fast and efficient nation, Singapore also prides itself on being a clean and green city. This can be seen from the 30-odd parks and green belts distributed evenly in the city and suburban areas.

LEFT
Sungei Buloh Nature Reserve is a stopping point for various types of migratory birds and other wildlife.

TOP
Carefully constructed hides throughout the 87-hectare wetland reserve provide observation points for visitors.

Parks range from small green areas to large green belts that have jogging and cycling tracks, food and beverage establishments, ponds, amphitheatres, lakes, barbecue pits, holiday chalets and golf driving ranges.

In addition, there are nature parks such as Sungei Buloh where mangroves and wetland thrive with various birds and wildlife. Bukit Timah Nature Reserve is the largest track of rainforest in Singapore and is a favourite place for bird watching, cycling and trekking.

Flora

Singapore is home to about 2,697 plant species. In view of its tiny dimensions, the flora is considered one of the richest in the world.

Singapore has numerous native species, although many are extinct or endangered. The plants that are grown by many households include orchids, ferns and tropical fruit trees such as rambutan and papaya. Plants such as chilli and pandan, which are popular ingredients in local gastronomy, are also common in households.

TOP LEFT & RIGHT
Coconut trees and huts are still left intact at Pulau Ubin, a rustic island getaway to the north of Singapore.

RIGHT
The Bukit Timah Nature Reserve is only 12 km from the city centre, yet it contains more species of plants than the entire North American continent.

Rooftop Gardens

As land becomes scarce, Singapore is constantly looking towards the sky to beautify its surroundings. With the use of skyrise greening, Singapore's concrete structures have become new avenues for further greenery.

Rooftop gardens have been developed on commercial buildings, hotels, private developments, government buildings and car parks of HDB estates. Other forms of high-rise greenery include extensive green roofs that are not designed for public use; greenery on the facades of buildings such as balconies, creepers on walls, planter boxes and mid level planting on intermediate levels and terraces; and decking over roads or canals that involve planting on other high-rise structures such as overhead bridges.

CLOCKWISE FROM TOP
This lush rooftop garden has a swimming pool to help its patrons to relax; Potted plants along corridors are a common sight in HDB blocks; The Singapore Orchid Gardens is home to 60,000 orchid plants; Pink bougainvilleas line many roads and are also grown as hanging plants from overhead bridges; White frangipanis produce a heady fragrance in tropical Singapore.

Botanical Gardens

The Botanical Gardens is a sprawling, 80-acre greenery that possesses an array of botanical and horticultural attractions. These have a rich history and a wonderful plant collection of worldwide significance. Complementing the native greenery are developments with educational and recreational facilities. The Botanical Gardens is also home to the Singapore Orchid Gardens, which houses the Vanda Miss Joaquim national flower.

LEFT
Schools regularly hold excursions to nature sites and other interesting places to allow students to learn hands-on.

TOP
Embellished metal gate at the entrance to the Singapore Botanic Gardens.

ABOVE
An old, gnarled tree sits in the Gardens.

SINGAPORE

TIMELINE

Jan 1819	**Sir Thomas Stamford Raffles lands on Singapore.**
1819–1942	**Under British rule, Singapore grows from a settlement to a colony.**
6 Feb 1819	**Founding of modern Singapore** Sir Stamford Raffles signs a treaty with Sultan Hussein to set Singapore as the new British base for the East India Company.
1826–1946	**Formation of the Straits Settlement** Singapore becomes part of the Straits Settlement with Penang and Malacca.
1942–1945	**Japanese Occupation** Singapore is renamed Syonan-To. This is a period of great hardship and suffering.
1945–1959	**Return to British rule** Rise of nationalism and political parties coupled with a rise in communism and racial disharmony.
1948–1960	**State of emergency** Communist insurgency
11 Dec 1950	**Maria Hertogh riots** Racial riots erupt over a Dutch girl who was adopted by a local Malay family.
6 Apr 1955	**First chief minister** David Marshall becomes the first chief minister in Singapore.
12 May 1955	**Hock Lee Bus riots** Bus workers riot over unsatisfactory working conditions.
1959–1963	**Self-government** The People's Action Party takes over with Prime Minister Lee Kuan Yew as leader and Yushof Ishak as the Yang di-Pertuan Negara (Head of State). Britain controls external affairs and defence.
1963–1965	**Merger with Malaysia** Singapore becomes part of Malaysia, which includes Sarawak and Sabah.
9 Aug 1965	**Independence** Singapore separates from Malaysia and becomes an independent state.
21 Sep 1965	**Singapore is admitted into the United Nations.**
22 Dec 1965	**Singapore declared a republic** Parliament passes a Constitution (Amendment) Act, making Singapore a republic and the Yang di-Pertuan Negara the president.

17 Aug 1967	**First intake of National Service men**
1967	**Formation of ASEAN** Singapore becomes a member of ASEAN.
13 Apr 1968	**First General Elections**
31 Oct 1971	**Singapore ceases to be a British military base.**
31 Mar 1975	**Dissolution of ANZUK Command** Australian and British forces leave Singapore for good.
29 Dec 1981	**Singapore Changi International Airport opens.**
1984	**Parliament receives its first two opposition members.**
1988	**Cellular phone service is introduced in Singapore.**
28 Nov 1990	**Lee Kuan Yew hands over the prime minister post to Goh Chok Tong. Lee Kuan Yew has been Singapore's prime minister since 1959.**
26–27 Mar 1991	**Singapore Airlines flight SQ117 is hijacked by terrorists. Commandos storm the aeroplane and kill all four terrorists in four minutes. All passengers and crew escape unhurt.**
2 Sep 1993	**First elected president** Up until 1994, presidents were appointed by the state. Ong Teng Cheong is the first president to be elected by Singaporeans.
20 Dec 1997	**SilkAir flight MI-185 plunges into Musi River in Palembang, Indonesia, and kills all 104 passengers and crew.**
1998	**Singapore joins other countries in the region in the Asian economic crisis, which began in 1997.**
31 Oct 2000	**Singapore Airlines aeroplane, flight SQ006, crashes in Taipei, Taiwan, amidst a typhoon and kills 83 people on board.**
Mar 2003	**Singapore detects its first Severe Acute Respiratory Syndrome (SARS) case. A total of 32 people in the country died of SARS.**
30 May 2003	**World Health Organisation declares Singapore a SARS-free country.**

LISTINGS

Boat Quay
Opening hours: From 11 am onwards
Getting there: Alight at Raffles Place
MRT Station.

Bukit Timah Nature Reserve
Hindhede Drive
Getting there: Take bus 171 from
Newton MRT Station.

Central Business District
Shenton Way
Getting there: Alight at either Raffles
Place or Tanjong Pagar MRT Station.

Clarke Quay
3 River Valley Road
Opening hours: From 11 am onwards
Getting there: Take bus 32 or 195 from
opposite Peninsula Plaza at City Hall
MRT station or take the river taxi from
Raffles Place MRT station.

Chijmes
Victoria Street
Opening hours: From 11 am onwards
Getting there: Alight at City Hall
MRT Station.

Chinatown
Eu Tong Sen Street
Getting there: Alight at Outram Park
MRT Station.

Escape Theme Park
Pasir Ris Close
Opening hours: Weekdays 4 pm–10
pm. Tuesdays, weekends and public
holidays 10 am–10 pm
Admission fee: Adult S$16, child S$8
Getting there: Take bus 354, 357 or
358 from Pasir Ris MRT Station.

Esplanade – Theatres on the Bay
Raffles Avenue
Getting there: Alight at City Hall
MRT Station.

Geylang Serai
Sims Avenue, Changi Road, Tanjong
Katong Road, Jalan Ubi
Getting there: Alight at Paya Lebar
MRT Station.

Goodwood Park Hotel
Scotts Road
Getting there: Two-minute walk from
Orchard Road

Jurong BirdPark
Jalan Ahmad Ibrahim
Getting there: Take bus 251 or 194
from Boon Lay MRT Station.
Admission fee: Adult S$12, child S$5
Opening hours: 9 am–6 pm daily

**Jurong Crocodile and
Reptile Paradise**
Jalan Ahmad Ibrahim
Admission fee: Adult S$8, child S$7.50
Opening hours: 9 am–6 pm daily
Getting there: See Jurong BirdPark

Lau Pa Sat Festival Market
Shenton Way
Opening hours: 24 hours daily
Getting there: Alight at Raffles Place
MRT Station.

Little India
Serangoon Road
Getting there: Alight at Dhoby Ghaut or
Bugis MRT Station.

Merlion Park
Fullerton Road
Getting there: Alight at Raffles Place
MRT Station.

Night Safari
Mandai Lake Road
Opening hours: 7.30 pm–12 midnight
Admission fee: Adult S$15.60,
child S$10.40
Getting there: From Ang Mo Kio MRT
Station, take bus 138. From Choa Chu
Kang MRT Station, take bus 927.

Prima Towers Pte Ltd
Telok Blangah Road
Opening hours: 11 am–3 pm and
6.30 pm–11 pm
Getting there: Take bus 97 from
Tanjong Pagar MRT Station.

Raffles Hotel
Beach Road
Getting there: Alight at City Hall
MRT station.

Sentosa Island
Opening hours: 24 hours daily
Admission fee: Adult S$6, child $4
Getting there: Take the cable car
from the Cable Car Towers.
Alternatively take the Sentosa
buses from Tiong Bahru MRT
Station or World Trade Centre.

**Singapore Botanic Gardens /
Singapore Orchid Gardens**
Cluny Road
Opening hours: 5 am–12 midnight
Admission fee: Free
Getting there: Take bus 7, 106 or 174
from Orchard Road.

Singapore Discovery Centre
Upper Jurong Road
Opening hours: 9 am–7 pm
from Tuesday to Sunday and on
public holidays
Admission fee: Adult S$9, child S$5
Getting there: Take bus 193 from Boon
Lay MRT Station.

Singapore Science Centre
Science Centre Road, Jurong
Opening hours: 10 am–6 pm
from Tuesday to Sunday and on
public holidays
Admission fee: Adult S$6, child S$3
Getting there: Take bus 335 from
Jurong East MRT Station.

Singapore Zoological Gardens
Mandai Lake Road
Opening hours: 8.30 am–6 pm daily
Admission fee: Adult S$12, child S$5
Getting there: See Night Safari

Sri Mariamman Temple
South Bridge Road
Getting there: Take buses 51, 61, 80,
103, 124, 145, 603, 851, 961 from
City Hall MRT Station.

Sultan Mosque
North Bridge Road
Getting there: Alight at Bugis
MRT Station.

Sungei Buloh Nature Park
Neo Tiew Crescent
Opening hours: 7.30 am–
7 pm on weekdays, 7 am–7 pm
on weekends and public holidays
Admission fee: Adult S$1, child/senior
citizen/student S$0.50
Getting there: Take bus 925 from
Kranji MRT Station.

Swissotel The Stamford
Stamford Road
Getting there: Alight at City Hall
MRT Station.

The Istana/The Istana Park
Orchard Road
Park opening hours: 8.30 am–6.30
pm daily
Admission fee: Free
Getting there: Alight at Dhoby
Ghaut MRT Station.

Thian Hock Keng Temple
Telok Ayer Street
Getting there: Take bus 186 from
Tanjong Pagar MRT Station.

Underwater World
Sentosa Island
Opening hours: 9 am–9 pm daily
Admission fee: Adult S$17, child S$11
Getting there: See Sentosa Island

Victoria Theatre & Concert Hall
Empress Place
Getting there: Alight at Raffles Place
MRT Station.

ADDITIONAL INFORMATION

Further Reading

Singapore 2002, Ministry of Information, Communication and the Arts (MITA), December 2001.
Singapore's Heritage Through Places of Historic Interest, Dhoraisingam Samuel, Elixir Consultancy Service, 1991.
Transitlink Guide 2002, Transit Link Pte Ltd, 2001.
Yearbook of Statistics Singapore 2002, Singapore Department of Statistics 2002.
Census of Population 2000: Administrative Report, Leow Bee Geok, Singapore Department of Statistics, 2002
Where Singapore, AsiaCity Publishing, January 2003 edition.
This Week Singapore, TTG Asia Media Pte Ltd, 4-10 January 2003 edition.
The Map of Singapore, TTG Asia Media Pte Ltd, 2002 Issue 96.11.
Survey on Infocomm Usage in Households 2000, Infocomm Development Authority of Singapore, August 2001.
The Concise Flora of Singapore: Gymnosperms & Dicotyledons, Hsuan Keng, Singapore University Press, 1990.
The Arts in Singapore Directory & Guide 1996, Accent Communications and the National Arts Council, 1996.

Websites

Changi International Airport: www.changiairport.com.sg
Department of Statistics Singapore: www.singstat.gov.sg
Economic Development Board Singapore: www.edb.gov.sg
Great Singapore Sale: www.greatsingaporesale.com.sg
Housing and Development Board: www.hdb.gov.sg
Infocomm Development Authority of Singapore: www.ida.gov.sg
International Movie Database: www.imdb.com
Land Transport Authority: www.lta.gov.sg
Maritime Port Authority: www.mpa.gov.sg
Media Development Authority: www.mda.gov.sg
Ministry of Education: www.moe.edu.sg
Ministry of Information, Communications and the Arts: www.mita.gov.sg
Ministry of Manpower: www.mom.gov.sg
Motor Traders Association of Singapore: www.mta.org.sg
National Arts Council: www.nac.gov.sg
National Parks Board: www.nparks.gov.sg
People's Action Party: www.pap.org.sg
Radio Singapore International: www.rsi.com.sg
Singapore Arts Festival: www.singaporeartsfest.com
Singapore Food Festival: www.singaporefoodfestival.com.sg
Singapore Infomap: www.sg
Singapore International Airlines: www.sia.com.sg
Singapore International Film Festival: www.filmfest.org.sg
Singapore River Buskers Festival: www.singapore-buskers.com
Singapore Sports Council: www.ssc.gov.sg
The Literature, Culture and Society of Singapore: www.scholars.nus.edu.sg
The Singapore Government, www.gov.sg
Womad Singapore: www.womadsingapore.com

Picture credits

AFP: 24 (queue), 31, 35 (wireless surf zone & Internet cafe), 41 (Esplanade), 52 (Womad).

Bes Stock: cover

Ch'ng Eu Lee: 18, 36 (Chijmes).

Eyepress: 29 (Stephanie Sun).

Getforme: 53 (Chingay).

HBL Network Photo Agency: 7, 9 (flag & merlion),10 (Raffles Hotel), 35 (Caucasian), 45 (sculpture).

Hans Hayden: 3 (children), 16 (both), 46, 57 (crowd), 59 (food court), 61 (fishball noodle).

Lim Hee Peng: 15.

Gilles Massot: 3 (man), 4, 5 (CBD), 11 (Esplanade — both images), 13, 17 (Malays & elderly ladies), 20, 21, 22, 23 (both), 26 (HDB block), 30, 32 (medical hall & CityLink Mall), 33 (Orchard Road), 34, 35 (Little India), 38, 40 (cafe), 41 (Boat Quay), 42, 43 (bird), 44, 48 (lanterns), 50, 51(both), 52 (Vesak Day), 56, 57 (satay), 58, 59 (durians & rambutans), 62 (cookies), 69 (Orchid Gardens), 70, back cover.

National Parks Board: 69 (rooftop garden).

PIONEER magazine: 26 (army).

Singapore Tourism Board: 3 (windsailing), 8 (both), 9 (orchids), 25 (parade), 27, 28, 29 (train), 33 (Orchard Road stalls), 36 (MacRitchie Reservoir), 37 (all), 39 (orchestra), 40 (picnic), 43 (tigers), 45 (museum & skydiving simulation), 47, 48 (candles), 49 (both), 52 (Christmas light-up), 53 (Singapore Food Festival), 54, 55 (food court), 60 (both), 61 (chilli crab, nasi lemak & tandoori chicken), 62 (raw fish salad), 63 (both), 64, 66, 67, 68 (both), 71 (both), 78.

Straits Times: 6 (all).

Susan Jane Manuel: 25 (kindergarten students).

Temasek Polytechnic: 25 (polytechnic students)

Times Editions Pte Ltd: 24 (t-shirt), 55 (hawker centre), 61 (chicken rice)

Benjamin Yap: 5 (Raffles), 10 (Victoria Memorial Hall), 11(Chijmes & Goodwood), 12, 14, 17 (Peranakans), 35 (baskets), 69 (frangipanis, bougainvilleas & corridor).

Yu Hui Ying: 29 (vehicles & Zoe Tay), 32 (CBD), 39 (play).